Women and Business

Transform your Emotions to financial gain

Rose C. Brian

Table of Contents

introduction

In the domain of abundance creation, the spotlight frequently gleams on systems, examination, and market patterns. However, in the midst of the ocean of numbers and graphs lies a secret fortune ready to be uncovered — the significant impact of our feelings. Welcome to "Change Your Feelings to Monetary Benefit," where we set out on an elating investigation of how tackling the force of feelings can make ready to uncommon monetary achievement.

Envision an existence where dread turns into a venturing stone to a valuable open door, where energy lights productive endeavors, and where versatility changes misfortunes into springboards for development. In these pages, we dig profound into the unpredictable connection between our feelings and our monetary undertakings. From excelling at the ability to appreciate people on a profound level to exploring the tempestuous waters of market unpredictability, this book fills in as your believed friend in opening the key to reasonable flourishing.

Plan to leave on a journey where dread changes into an open door, where enthusiasm fills productivity, and where disappointment turns into the foundation of development.

Chapter 1

Grasping the Force of Feelings in Monetary Achievement

In the realm of money, achievement frequently appears to be a numbers game — a domain represented by information, calculations, and market patterns. In any case, underneath the surface lies a strong power that can represent the deciding moment even the most carefully made methodologies: our emoti

The Connection Among Feelings and Funds

delight can prompt hasty spending, amassing obligation, and dismissing long haul monetary objectives. These feelings frequently emerge from cultural tensions, promoting strategies, and the need to stay aware of others. By dominating persistence and postponed satisfaction, we can pursue better monetary decisions that line up with our needs.

Feelings significantly affect our way of behaving, independent direction, and by and large prosperity. With regards to funds, feelings can either enable us or upset our advancement. We should investigate how various feelings might impact our monetary decisions:

• Dread and Uneasiness: Dread and uneasiness can prompt silly direction, for example, indiscreetly selling speculations during a market slump or keeping away from important dangers. These feelings frequently come from an apprehension about disappointment, misfortune, or vulnerability. By figuring out how to oversee dread and uneasiness, we can move toward monetary choices all the more impartially and reasonably.

Covetousness and Presumptuousness

Covetousness and presumptuousness can prompt unnecessary gamble taking, like putting resources into theoretical endeavors or overstretching oneself monetarily. These feelings frequently emerge when people experience achievement or see others benefitting from specific open doors. By overseeing voracity and presumptuousness, we can keep a decent and reasonable way to deal with our funds.

Fretfulness and Moment Satisfaction

Fretfulness and the craving for moment satisfaction can prompt imprudent spending, amassing obligation, and dismissing long haul monetary objectives. These feelings frequently emerge from cultural tensions, promoting strategies, and the need to stay aware of others. By dominating tolerance and deferred delight, we can pursue better monetary decisions that line up with our needs.

Example: You might feel the strain to update your way of life or buy the most recent contraptions. Rather than surrendering to hasty getting, you can rehearse deferred delight by laying out monetary objectives, making a spending plan, and setting aside cash towards those objectives. This permits you to focus on your drawn out monetary accomplishment over momentary longings.

Functional Methods for Dealing with Feelings and Making Monetary Progress

Now that we comprehend the effect of feelings on our monetary excursion, how about we investigate a few reasonable tips to assist us with dealing with our feelings successfully:

Increment Profound Mindfulness

Begin by turning out to be more mindful of your feelings and how they impact your monetary choices. Carve out opportunity to think about your ways of behaving, examples, and triggers. This mindfulness will help you perceive and address any close to home road obstructions that prevent your monetary achievement.

•Practice Care and Reflection

Care and reflection are strong methods to develop close to home equilibrium and decrease pressure. Put away devoted time every day to rehearse care or participate in contemplation. These practices will assist you with remaining present, pursue better choices, and foster a positive outlook towards your monetary objectives.

•Construct a Strong Organization

Encircle yourself with people who share comparable monetary desires and values. A steady organization can give support, direction, and responsibility on your excursion towards monetary achievement. Participate in conversations, go to courses or join online networks that encourage solid monetary discussions.

•Instruct Yourself

Persistently teach yourself about individual budget, financial planning, and cash the executives. The more information you have, the more sure and engaged you will become in settling on informed monetary choices. Understand books, pay attention to webcasts, and follow respectable monetary specialists to extend your monetary education.

Chapter 2

Mastering Emotional Intelligence For Wealth Creation

Dominating capacity to appreciate people on a deeper level for abundance creation includes utilizing your feelings and understanding those of others to go with informed choices, construct connections, and make monetary progress. Here is an extensive outline:

Grasping Capacity to understand anyone at their core (EI)

The capacity to understand people on a profound level incorporates mindfulness, self-guideline, social mindfulness, and relationship the executives.

-Mindfulness includes perceiving your own feelings, assets, shortcomings, and their effect on your monetary choices.

-Self-guideline is the capacity to deal with your feelings, driving forces, and responses, particularly during high-stress monetary circumstances.

- Social mindfulness is understanding the feelings and requirements of others, which is pivotal for systems administration, discussion, and cooperation.

-Relationship the executives includes really imparting, settling clashes, and creating useful connections to upgrade financial momentum creation potential open doors.

The capacity to understand anyone at their core in Monetary Navigation

Feelings frequently impact monetary choices, like money management, spending, and hazard taking.

-Dominating capacity to appreciate people on a profound level assists people with pursuing judicious monetary choices by perceiving and dealing with close to home inclinations like trepidation, covetousness, and presumptuousness.

- It empowers people to evaluate gambles impartially, control incautious way of behaving, and try not to pursue choices exclusively founded on feelings.

Building Versatility and Adapting to Failure:

- Monetary undertakings imply dangers, vulnerabilities, and misfortunes. Dominating ability to understand people at their core outfits people with flexibility to return from disappointments and mishaps.

- It helps in rethinking disappointments as learning open doors, overseeing pressure, and keeping up with center around long haul monetary objectives in spite of impermanent mishaps.

Compelling Correspondence and Discussion

- The capacity to understand people on a deeper level assumes a critical part in successful correspondence and discussion, fundamental abilities for abundance creation.

- It includes undivided attention, compassion, and understanding the points of view of others, whether it's arranging bargains, overseeing client connections, or teaming up with colleagues.

Building and Driving High-Performing Groups

- Fruitful abundance creation frequently requires collaboration and administration. The ability to understand people on a deeper level is fundamental for building strong groups and rousing others to accomplish normal monetary objectives.

- Successful pioneers with high ability to appreciate individuals at their core can propel, engage, and support colleagues, prompting expanded efficiency and advancement.

Systems administration and Relationship Building

- Connections are principal in abundance creation, whether it's with financial backers, clients, or colleagues.

The ability to appreciate people on a profound level aides in building and keeping up serious areas of strength for with, based connections.

- It includes sympathy, relational abilities, and the capacity to comprehend and address the issues of others, encouraging commonly helpful associations that can prompt monetary open doors.

Ceaseless Learning and Self-Advancement

- Dominating capacity to appreciate people at their core for abundance creation is a continuous cycle that requires ceaseless learning and self-improvement.

- It includes looking for criticism, pondering encounters, and effectively dealing with further developing capacity to appreciate anyone at their core abilities to adjust to changing monetary scenes and self-improvement.

In synopsis, dominating ability to appreciate people on a profound level for abundance creation includes understanding and dealing with feelings really, building solid connections, settling on objective monetary choices, and constantly creating fundamental abilities for outcome in the steadily developing monetary world.

Chapter 3

The monetary blueprint

In this crucial part, we shift our concentration from understanding the job of feelings to making a hearty monetary blueprint. Like a gifted specialist outlining a front line, we investigate the fundamental components of a fruitful monetary methodology.

From defining clear objectives and goals to planning a customized venture guide, we dive into the means important to construct a strong starting point for monetary achievement. We examine the significance of planning, saving, and contributing astutely, featuring the key rules that structure the foundation of any viable monetary arrangement.

Additionally, we address the basic part of chance administration, underscoring the need to offset expected gets back with the inborn vulnerabilities of the market. By contriving techniques to relieve gambles and safeguard our monetary advantages, we defend our riches and prepare for long haul success.

•Components of a fruitful monetary system

A fruitful monetary system normally incorporates:

•Clear Objectives: Characterize your present moment and long haul monetary goals.

• Planning: Make a spending plan to oversee expenses and dispense reserves successfully.

•.Reserve funds: Routinely save and contribute for future necessities and crises.

• Obligation The executives: Foster an arrangement to really oversee and pay off past commitments.

•Broadened Ventures: Put resources into a blend of resources for spread risk and boost returns.

•Retirement Arranging: Save for retirement through annuity plans, IRAs, or other retirement accounts.

• Normal Survey: Occasionally audit and change your monetary arrangement in light of changes in objectives, pay, or economic situation.

Chapter 4

Mastering The Act Of Money

Dominating the demonstration of cash goes past acquiring it; it envelops different parts of monetary administration, mentality, and conduct. Here is a complete outline:

•Monetary Literacy

Understanding fundamental monetary ideas, for example, planning, saving, financial planning, obligation the board, and retirement arranging is fundamental.

Dominating monetary proficiency includes instructing oneself through books, courses, studios, and looking for guidance from monetary experts.

•Planning and Monetary Planning

Making a spending plan includes following pay and costs to guarantee that spending lines up with monetary objectives.

Dominating planning requires defining reasonable monetary objectives, focusing on spending, and changing the financial plan as conditions change.

•Saving and Investing

Setting aside includes saving cash for transient objectives and crises, while putting includes placing cash into resources with the assumption for creating returns over the long haul.

Dominating saving and contributing includes grasping different venture choices, risk resilience, and enhancement to create financial momentum consistently over the long run.

•Obligation Management

Overseeing obligation really includes figuring out various kinds of obligation, for example, charge card obligation, understudy loans, and home loans, and creating systems to productively take care of obligation.

Dominating obligation the executives incorporates focusing on exorbitant premium obligation, arranging lower loan fees, and staying away from pointless obligation whenever the situation allows.

•Monetary Attitude and Behavior

Fostering a solid monetary outlook includes changing convictions and perspectives towards cash, for example, conquering shortage attitude, developing a mentality of overflow, and embracing monetary obligation.

Dominating monetary way of behaving incorporates rehearsing discipline, deferred satisfaction, and staying away from incautious spending to accomplish long haul monetary objectives.

•Risk The board and Insurance

Understanding and relieving monetary dangers is vital for safeguarding resources and accomplishing monetary security.

Dominating gamble the board includes having fitting protection inclusion for wellbeing, life, property, and obligation chances, as well as broadening speculations to limit openness to showcase vacillations.

•Procuring and Expanding Income

Dominating the demonstration of cash includes overseeing existing assets as well as tracking down ways of expanding pay.

This might include progressing in one's vocation, beginning a side business, putting resources into training or abilities improvement, or looking for recurring sources of income, for example, land or profit paying ventures.

•Long haul Abundance Building

Creating long haul financial momentum requires an essential methodology that integrates saving, effective money management, and making arrangements for retirement.

Dominating long haul growing a strong financial foundation includes putting forth clear monetary objectives, routinely looking into and changing monetary plans, and remaining restrained and patient during market vacillations.

•Liberality and Giving

Dominating the demonstration of cash likewise includes perceiving the significance of offering in return and being liberal with assets.

Whether through magnanimous gifts, chipping in time and abilities, or supporting causes that line up with individual qualities, giving can bring satisfaction and have a beneficial outcome on networks and society all in all.

Women, feelings and cash

The connection between ladies, feelings, and cash is multi-layered, affected by cultural standards, individual encounters, and mental elements. Here is an investigation of this complicated relationship:

*Social Molding and Orientation Roles**:

By and large, ladies have frequently been related with close to home characteristics, for example, sustaining, sympathy, and awareness, while men have been connected to levelheadedness, confidence, and hazard taking in monetary issues.

Cultural standards and orientation jobs can shape ladies' perspectives towards cash, prompting convictions that they might be less skilled or keen on overseeing funds really.

*The capacity to appreciate anyone on a profound level and Monetary Choice Making**:

*The ability to appreciate anyone at their core and Monetary Choice Making**:

- Ladies will generally score higher in capacity to appreciate anyone at their core than men, which can be profitable in monetary direction.

- The capacity to understand people on a profound level empowers ladies to perceive and deal with their feelings successfully, prompting more smart and informed monetary decisions.

- Be that as it may, feelings can likewise cloud judgment, prompting hasty spending, evasion of monetary preparation, or hesitance to pursue takes a chance in venture open doors.

Cash and Self-Worth

- For certain ladies, there might be areas of strength for an association between their self-esteem and monetary achievement or freedom.

- Accomplishing monetary objectives can support certainty and confidence, while monetary battles or reliance might prompt insecurities or stress.

- Ladies frequently shuffle numerous jobs, like parental figures, providers, and experts, which can influence their monetary choices and needs.

- Adjusting family needs, profession yearnings, and individual objectives can inspire a scope of feelings, impacting decisions connected with spending, saving, and financial planning.

Exploring Orientation Pay Hole and Monetary Inequality

- The orientation pay hole and foundational obstructions can add to monetary difficulties for ladies, influencing their acquiring potential, retirement reserve funds, and generally monetary security.

- Managing monetary imbalance can bring out sensations of dissatisfaction, outrage, or vulnerability, inciting ladies to advocate for equivalent open doors and monetary strengthening.

Steady Organizations and Monetary Education

- Building steady organizations and getting to monetary schooling are essential for ladies to acquire certainty and ability in overseeing cash.

- Mentorship, peer support, and designated monetary education projects can furnish ladies with the information and assets to actually explore monetary choices.

Social and Relational Dynamics**:

- Social assumptions and relational intricacies might impact ladies' jobs and obligations in regards to cash the executives.

- Open correspondence and cooperation with accomplices, relatives, or monetary experts can assist ladies with tending to close to home boundaries and pursue informed monetary decisions.

Strengthening and Monetary Independence**:

- Accomplishing monetary autonomy and independence can be engaging for ladies, encouraging a feeling of opportunity, security, and command over their lives.

- Defeating close to home boundaries, testing cultural standards, and upholding for equivalent open doors are fundamental stages towards accomplishing monetary strengthening.

Chapter 5

Plan Like A Star

Arranging like a star in business includes careful readiness, vital reasoning, and compelling execution. This is the way to make it happen:

Put forth Clear Objectives and Targets

- Characterize explicit, quantifiable, feasible, important, and time-bound (Brilliant) objectives for your business.

- Separate long haul goals into more modest, significant achievements to actually follow progress.

Lead Exhaustive Market Research

Comprehend your objective market, including socioeconomics, inclinations, needs, and patterns.

Break down contenders to recognize qualities, shortcomings, potential open doors, and dangers (SWOT investigation).

Foster an Itemized Business Plan**:

Frame your plan of action, including items or administrations, target market, incentive, income streams, and appropriation channels.

Make monetary projections, including deals estimates, costs, and income proclamations.

Incorporate alternate courses of action to address likely dangers and difficulties.

*Construct Areas of strength for a:

Enlist gifted people with assorted abilities and encounters to supplement your assets.

Obviously characterize jobs and obligations to guarantee everybody grasps their commitment to the business' prosperity.

Cultivate a positive work culture that empowers coordinated effort, development, and persistent improvement.

Carry out Successful Advertising Strategies**:

Foster an extensive promoting plan that integrates on the web and disconnected techniques to arrive at your interest group.

Use computerized showcasing instruments, for example, virtual entertainment, content advertising, email missions, and website streamlining (Web optimization) to increment brand perceivability and client commitment.

Screen promoting execution measurements and change techniques in light of criticism and results.

Oversee Funds Wisely:

Make a definite financial plan that designates assets effectively and tracks costs.

Screen income routinely to guarantee there is sufficient liquidity to cover functional costs and speculation needs.

- Consider looking for monetary guidance from experts or utilizing bookkeeping programming to smooth out monetary administration processes.

Center around Client Experience**:

Focus on consumer loyalty by conveying top notch items or administrations and giving uncommon client assistance.

Accumulate criticism from clients to recognize regions for development and address any issues expeditiously.

Assemble long haul associations with clients through customized collaborations and dedication programs.

Adjust and Innovate

Remain coordinated and adaptable to adjust to changing economic situations, customer inclinations, and innovative progressions.

Cultivate a culture of development by empowering imagination, trial and error, and chance taking inside the association.

Screen industry patterns and contender exercises to distinguish new open doors for development and advancement.

*Screen Progress and Change Strategies

Consistently audit key execution pointers (KPIs) and measurements to assess the viability of your business techniques.

Recognize areas of progress and make important acclimations to upgrade execution and accomplish your business objectives.

Remain proactive and receptive to changes in the business climate to keep an upper hand.

By following these means and embracing a proactive and key way to deal with arranging, you can situate your business for progress and successfully explore difficulties and potential open doors in the commercial center.

Chapter 6

Transform Failure Into Growth

Changing disappointment into development is a strong mentality that empowers people to gain from mishaps, adjust, and at last make progress. Here are a few significant illustrations that can be gathered from misfortunes

1.Embrace Disappointment as a Learning Opportunity

- Rather than review disappointment as a mishap, see it as a significant opportunity for growth.

Break down what turned out badly, recognize regions for development, and concentrate key examples that can be applied to future undertakings.

2. Construct Flexibility and Persistence

- Disappointment tests your strength and assurance. Use difficulties as a chance to fortify your purpose and diligence.

Recall that achievement is much of the time the aftereffect of flexibility and the capacity to return from misfortune.

3. Refine Your Techniques and Approach

Misfortunes give bits of knowledge into what procedures and approaches may not be working.

- Utilize this information to refine your strategies, explore different avenues regarding novel thoughts, and adjust your way to deal with better line up with your objectives.

4. Foster a Development Mindset

Take on a development outlook, accepting that capacities and insight can be created through commitment and difficult work.

View misfortunes as impermanent snags on the way to development and improvement, as opposed to fixed restrictions.

5.Look for Criticism and Support

Make sure to criticism from coaches, peers, or confided in counselors.

Encircle yourself with a steady organization that can offer direction, consolation, and valuable analysis to assist you with exploring difficulties.

6. Remain Adaptable and Open-Minded

- Be available to elective points of view and groundbreaking thoughts.

Remain adaptable in your methodology, ready to adjust and turn whenever important to conquer obstructions and quickly take advantage of chances.

7. Develop Self-Compassion

Practice self-sympathy and thoughtfulness towards yourself during seasons of disappointment.

- Perceive that mishaps are a characteristic piece of the excursion towards progress and indulge yourself with a similar sympathy and understanding you would propose to others confronting comparative difficulties.

8. Center around Arrangements, Not Blame

Rather than harping on who or what is to be faulted for the disappointment, center around tracking down arrangements and pushing ahead.

- Take responsibility for botches, yet additionally perceive that disappointment is much of the time the consequence of different elements, large numbers of which might be outside of your reach

9.Observe Progress and Little Wins**:

 Recognize and praise your advancement, regardless of how little.

Perceive that development is a continuous cycle, and each forward-moving step, regardless of how gradual, carries you nearer to your objectives.

By incorporating these examples and taking on a development situated outlook, people can change disappointment into a chance for individual and expert development, flexibility, and eventually, achievement.

www.ingramcontent.com/pod-product-compliance
Lightning Source LLC
Chambersburg PA
CBHW051923250726
48659CB00002B/804